from SEA TO SHINING SEA
WYOMING

By Dennis Brindell Fradin and Judith Bloom Fradin

CONSULTANTS

Philip Roberts, J.D., Ph.D., Assistant Professor, Department of History,
University of Wyoming, Laramie

Robert L. Hillerich, Ph.D., Professor Emeritus, Bowling Green State University;
Consultant, Pinellas County Schools, Florida

CHILDRENS PRESS®
CHICAGO

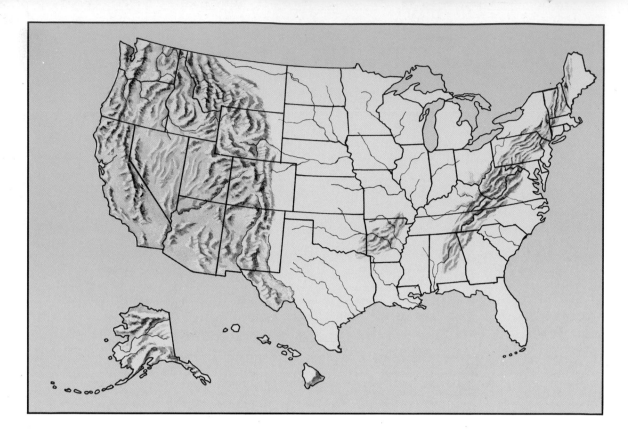

Wyoming is one of the six Rocky Mountain states. The other Rocky Mountain states are Colorado, Idaho, Montana, Nevada, and Utah.

For our friends, the Goers: Dick, Ellie, Eric, Peter, Jon, and Beth

For her help, the authors thank Ann Nelson, senior historian, Historical Research, Wyoming State Museum

Front cover picture, Grand Teton National Park; page 1, a farm north of Cheyenne; back cover, State Capitol, Cheyenne

Project Editor: Joan Downing
Design Director: Karen Kohn
Typesetting: Graphic Connections, Inc.
Engraving: Liberty Photoengraving

39999023835414

Library of Congress Cataloging-in-Publication Data

Fradin, Dennis B.
  Wyoming / by Dennis Brindell Fradin and Judith Bloom Fradin.
    p.   cm. — (From sea to shining sea)
  Includes index.
  ISBN 0-516-03850-8
  1. Wyoming—Juvenile literature. [1. Wyoming.]
I. Fradin, Judith Bloom. II. Title. III. Series: Fradin,
Dennis B. From sea to shining sea.
F761.3.F68   1994   93-39880
978.7—dc20   CIP
                                            AC

Table of Contents

Lunch Counter Rapids on the Snake River at Jackson Hole

INTRODUCING THE EQUALITY STATE

Wyoming was the first state to grant women full voting rights. That is why it is called the "Equality State." Wyoming is also known for its cowboys. Some people call it the "Cowboy State."

A cowboy on a bucking bronco is pictured on Wyoming license plates.

Wyoming is a large western state. Its name means "large plains." The Great Plains meet the Rocky Mountains in Wyoming.

Beautiful scenery fills the state. The rugged ranges of the Rockies twist through Wyoming. The Tetons are among the world's loveliest mountains. Hot waters called geysers shoot upward in Yellowstone National Park. Waterfalls tumble downward along Wyoming's rivers.

Wyoming leads the other states at mining coal. It also has large oil deposits. The state is also a big cattle, sheep, and wool producer.

Wyoming is special in other ways. Where is the country's oldest national park? What state had the country's first woman governor? What state has the fewest people? Where were artist Jackson Pollock and author Patricia MacLachlan born? The answer to these questions is: Wyoming!

A picture map
of Wyoming

Overleaf: The
Absaroka Mountains
form a background for
red rock formations in
Wyoming's badlands.

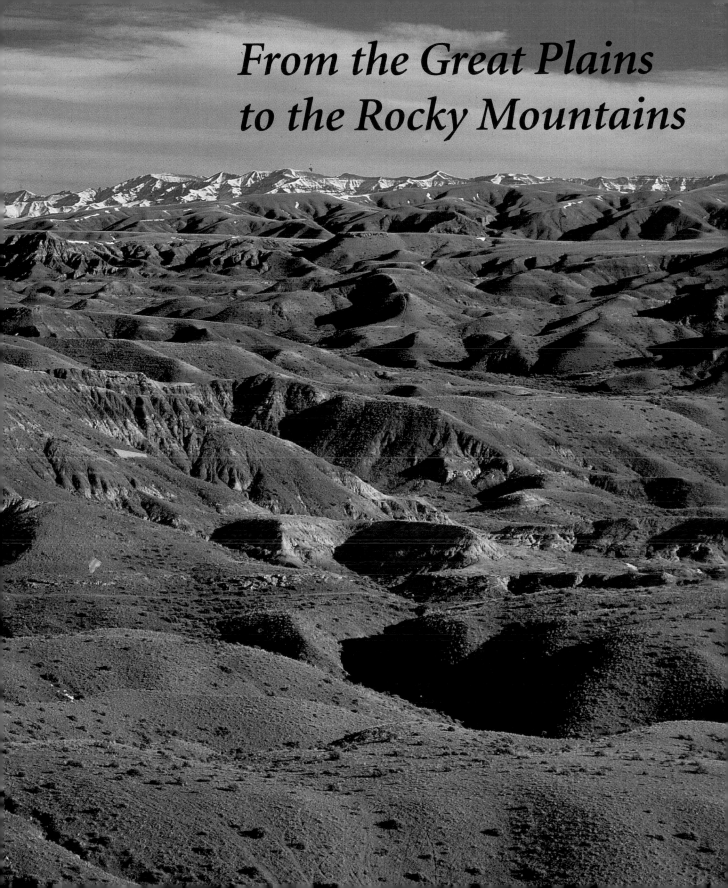

From the Great Plains
to the Rocky Mountains

From the Great Plains to the Rocky Mountains

Wyoming is a near-perfect rectangle. The state covers 97,809 square miles. It is the ninth largest of the fifty states. The Rocky Mountains run through much of Wyoming. That makes it one of the six Rocky Mountain states. Four other Rocky Mountain states form part of Wyoming's border. Montana is to the north and west. Idaho and Utah are to the west. Utah and Colorado lie to the south. South Dakota and Nebraska are to the east.

Wyoming has three major land areas. The Great Plains cover part of eastern Wyoming. This is flat land with short grasses. It is good for sheep and cattle to graze on. Wheat, corn, and sugar beets are also grown on the plains.

The Rocky Mountains rise above western and central Wyoming. The Rockies help make Wyoming the second-highest state. Wyoming land averages 6,700 feet above sea level. Wyoming's highest point is Gannett Peak. This mountain towers 13,804 feet above sea level. That is 2.5 miles high.

Intermontane basins are the third land area. They are flat lands between the mountains. Sheep

High plains at the base of the Bighorn Mountains

Only Colorado has a higher average elevation than Wyoming. It averages 6,800 feet above sea level.

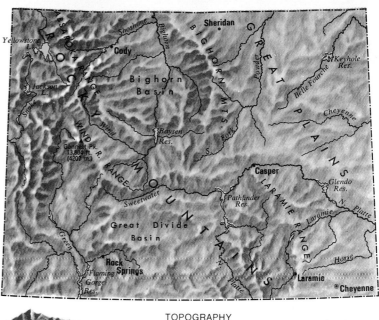

TOPOGRAPHY

| 5,000 m. | 2,000 m. | 1,000 m. | 500 m. | 200 m. | 100 m. | Sea | |
| 16,404 ft. | 6,562 ft. | 3,281 ft. | 1,640 ft. | 656 ft. | 328 ft. | Level | Below |

and cattle graze there. Much of Wyoming's mineral deposits are found under this land.

Left: Mirror Lake and cascade in the Snowy Range of the Medicine Bow Mountains

LAKES AND RIVERS

Many natural lakes lie in Wyoming's mountains. Yellowstone and Jackson lakes are the largest. The state also has a few large lakes created by damming rivers. They include Flaming Gorge and Buffalo Bill reservoirs.

The Continental Divide runs through western Wyoming. Rivers east of the divide flow into the Atlantic Ocean. Rivers to the west empty into the Pacific Ocean. Wyoming's North Platte, Powder, and Sweetwater rivers are east of the divide. The

9

*Wildflowers in
Yellowstone National
Park*

*Pronghorns are North
America's fastest
animals. They can run
at a speed of 70 miles
per hour. Mule deer
have big ears like those
of mules.*

Shoshone, Wind, Bighorn, Green, and Snake rivers are west of it.

WOODS AND WILDLIFE

One-sixth of Wyoming is wooded. The state has ten national forests. The cottonwood is the state tree. Pines, firs, and spruces are other trees. Quaking aspens also grow in Wyoming. They shake in the wind.

Many wildflowers bloom in Wyoming. The Indian paintbrush is the state flower. Evening stars, windflowers, buttercups, and five-fingers grow there, too.

About 3,500 buffalo live in Wyoming. The buffalo (American bison) is the state animal. One appears on Wyoming's flag. Wyoming also has about 400,000 pronghorn antelopes. That is more than any other state has. Mule deer live throughout the state. Elk and moose are other members of Wyoming's deer family. Bighorn sheep climb through Wyoming's highlands. Mountain lions hunt these wild sheep. Black bears, grizzly bears, beavers, rabbits, and coyotes are other Wyoming animals.

The meadowlark is the state bird. Its song sounds like a flute. Bald eagles and golden eagles soar above Wyoming. Swans, wild turkeys, grouse, ducks, and geese also fly about the state. Trout, bass, walleye, and perch swim in Wyoming's waters.

CLIMATE

Wyoming's climate is cool, sunny, and dry. Winter temperatures often dip below 0 degrees Fahrenheit. The state's record low was minus 63 degrees Fahrenheit. Wyoming's record high was 114 degrees Fahrenheit. But summer temperatures around 80 degrees Fahrenheit are more common. On summer days, the sun shines on Wyoming three-fourths of the time.

Wyoming receives little rain. Rainfall is about 5 inches in the lowlands. The mountains receive about 15 inches. Southeast Wyoming suffers hailstorms. An August 1985 storm piled up 3 feet of hail in Cheyenne. Winter snowstorms are common, too. Each year, the state's southeastern area receives about 6 feet of snow. About 20 feet of snow falls in the northwest mountains.

Wyoming is the windiest state. Its wind speeds average 13 miles per hour. Sometimes snowstorms driven by very high winds strike Wyoming. These storms are called blizzards.

Ice fishing is a favorite sport during Wyoming's cold winters.

Overleaf: Buffalo Bill Cody statue, in Cody

11

*From Ancient
Times Until
Today*

From Ancient Times Until Today

Millions of years ago, dinosaurs roamed across Wyoming. Stegosaurus and triceratops lived there. The longest dinosaur made its home there, too. This was the 100-foot diplodocus. Small animals also lived in Wyoming. Drinker nisti was the size of a turkey. Eohippus was a small horse. It was not much bigger than a rabbit.

American Indians

The first people reached Wyoming more than 12,000 years ago. They were ancestors of today's American Indians. These early Indians lived in caves. They hunted mammoths. Mammoths were huge, hairy animals related to today's elephants. In 1960-61, mammoth bones were found near Worland. Near the 11,000-year-old bones were ancient tools. Early Indians had made the tools.

Between 1,000 and 10,000 years ago, Indians built Medicine Wheel. It is in the Bighorn Mountains near Lovell. Medicine Wheel is made of rocks laid out like a huge wheel. The Indians might

These prehistoric herring fossils were found in the Green River area.

Left: Wyoming's early Indians made these petroglyphs, or rock carvings.
Right: A George Catlin painting of a buffalo hunt

have used it as a giant calendar. From it, they could tell the first day of each season. The sun lined up with the rocks in a certain way. The early Indians also carved and painted pictures on rocks. Rock carvings at Castle Gardens near Riverton are hundreds of years old.

Since the 1700s, many Indian groups have lived near Wyoming's rivers. The Shoshone lived in the Green River valley. The Crow were near the Bighorn River. Close to the Powder River were the Sioux. The Cheyenne and Arapaho lived south of the North Platte River. These American Indians hunted buffalo. They used the buffalo for food and clothing. They even made tents called tepees from buffalo hides.

14

European and American Explorers and Traders

Parts of present-day Wyoming were once claimed by Spain, France, and England. But no Spanish or English explorers ever went there. In 1743, François and Louis Joseph Vérendrye reached the Big Horn Mountains. These French-Canadian traders were looking for new sources of furs. They are thought to have been the first Europeans in Wyoming. But the Vérendrye brothers did no trading in Wyoming.

The furs were used to make hats and coats.

By 1732, England had thirteen colonies along the Atlantic Ocean. In 1776, those colonies declared their independence from England. They became known as the United States. In 1803, the United States bought France's last piece of North American land. This land was called the Louisiana Purchase. The United States paid France $15 million for it. Part of Wyoming was in the Louisiana Purchase. By 1848, all of present-day Wyoming belonged to the United States.

In 1804-06, Meriwether Lewis and William Clark explored much of the Louisiana Purchase. But they did not enter Wyoming. John Colter, a fur trapper, was in Lewis and Clark's party. He left the group to explore Wyoming. In 1807, Colter

Mountain man Jim Beckwourth

Rendezvous *means "meeting place."*

entered what is now Yellowstone National Park. He became the first non-Indian in this part of the country. In 1810, Colter went back East. He reported that Wyoming was rich in beavers and other fur-bearing animals.

Several hundred mountain men came to Wyoming. They roamed the mountains trapping animals. Others traded with the Indians for furs. Their life was dangerous and lonely. In 1823, a grizzly bear attacked Jedediah Smith in Wyoming. A companion sewed Smith's ear back on. Many mountain men lived with the Indians. Some married Indian women. Jim Beckwourth was a black mountain man. He lived with the Crow Indians in Wyoming.

William Ashley ran a fur company that worked in Wyoming. In 1825, Ashley hosted Wyoming's first *rendezvous*. This gathering of mountain men took place along Wyoming's Green River. The gathering became a yearly event. Indian men and women joined trappers and traders at the rendezvous. Furs and supplies were exchanged. There was plenty to eat and drink. The mountain men held shooting contests and horse races. They sang and danced. Then the men returned to the wilderness for another year.

16

In time, trading posts were built. Traders, trappers, and Indians met at these posts. In 1834, traders William Sublette and Robert Campbell built Fort William. It was Wyoming's first permanent non-Indian settlement. This later became Fort Laramie. In 1842, mountain man Jim Bridger and his business partner, Louis Vasquez, began Fort Bridger. It was in southwest Wyoming.

With forts as meeting places, the Wyoming rendezvous lost importance. The last rendezvous was held in 1840. By that time, the beaver supply had run low. Too many of them had been killed. The age of the mountain men ended around 1845.

This is one of the many restored buildings at the Fort Laramie National Historic Site.

PIONEER TRAILS AND INDIAN WARS

By 1840, Americans wanted to settle in the West. Wyoming became a place to pass through on the way farther west. In 1841, pioneers started heading to Oregon over the Oregon Trail. They traveled in long wagon trains. The Mormon Trail to Utah also went through Wyoming. So did the California Trail. All three trails led through South Pass. This was in southwest Wyoming. This pass through the mountains had been discovered by whites in 1812. Robert Stuart, a mountain man, had found it. The

These pioneers were traveling westward during the mid-1800s.

Overland Trail went across southern Wyoming. It joined the other trails at Fort Bridger.

At first, the Indians helped these travelers find food and water. By 1850, the pioneers had killed thousands of buffalo. This cut into the Indians' food supply. Fights broke out between the Indians and the pioneers.

The United States Army tried to keep the peace. In 1854, Lieutenant John Grattan, with twenty-nine soldiers, tried to arrest a Sioux. The man had killed a pioneer's cow. The arrest angered the Sioux. After all, white people had killed countless buffalo. The Sioux killed all thirty soldiers. This is known as the Grattan Massacre.

More battles followed. In 1865, Indians killed twenty-six soldiers in central Wyoming. The town of Casper was built near the battle site. It was named for Caspar Collins. He was one of the soldiers who died. (A spelling mistake changed the last a in his name to an e.)

Gold had been discovered in Montana in the 1860s. To help miners reach the goldfields, the Bozeman Trail was built. It cut through Indian hunting grounds in northern Wyoming. The Indians fought to protect their land. The army built forts to guard the trail.

Ruts made by thousands of pioneer wagons can still be seen at Oregon Trail Ruts National Historic Landmark, near Guernsey.

19

Sioux chief Red Cloud (third from right) and other Indian leaders signed peace treaties with the United States in 1868.

Two battles were fought near Fort Phil Kearny. The Fetterman Fight took place in 1866. Captain W. J. Fetterman and eighty-one men were killed. About two hundred Indians also died. The Wagon Box Fight occurred in 1867. Soldiers fought from behind overturned wagons. They killed more than six hundred Indians.

In 1868, Wyoming's Indians signed peace treaties with the United States government. In the Fort Laramie Treaty, the Bozeman Trail and its forts were closed. The Sioux and Cheyenne agreed not to try to stop railroad building in Wyoming. In the Fort Bridger Treaty, the Shoshone were given land in the Wind River valley. The Arapaho joined them there in 1877.

THE WYOMING TERRITORY

Gold was discovered at South Pass in 1867. Thousands of miners arrived. About fifteen mining camps sprang up. One camp became South Pass City. It soon had almost 4,000 people.

Wyoming's first railroad was the Union Pacific. It arrived in 1867-68. Six cities were built across southern Wyoming as the railroad came through.

Cities grew up along the railroads when they arrived in Wyoming in 1867-68.

Cheyenne as it looked in 1868.

Cheyenne was founded in 1867. Laramie was begun in 1868. Rawlins, Rock Springs, Green River, and Evanston were also begun in 1868.

Coal mines first opened in Wyoming in the 1860s. Coal fueled the railroads.

By 1868, Wyoming had several thousand settlers. On July 25, the United States Congress made Wyoming a territory. Cheyenne became Wyoming's capital in 1869.

William Bright proposed a bill in Wyoming's legislature in 1869. He was a lawmaker from South Pass City. The bill was for women's right to vote and to hold office. Bright's bill became law on

December 10, 1869. This was the first law of its kind in the United States.

Wyoming women soon exercised their rights. On February 17, 1870, Esther Morris became the country's first woman judge. She was from South Pass City. Eliza Swain of Laramie voted on September 6, 1870. She was the first woman to vote in a countrywide election. Also in Laramie, women first served on juries in 1870.

Wyoming Territory also had the country's first national park. Yellowstone National Park was founded in 1872.

Also in the 1870s, large cattle and sheep ranches sprang up in Wyoming. The grasslands were good for grazing livestock. By 1885, Wyoming was a leading raiser of both cattle and beef.

Trouble with the Indians started again in 1874. Gold had been discovered in the Black Hills. The Fort Laramie Treaty stated that no white people were to enter this land. Soon, miners were in the Black Hills. The Sioux and Cheyenne went to war. They wanted to protect their land.

The Indian wars ended in 1876. That November, United States troops attacked a Cheyenne village in northern Wyoming. The Indians fled on foot to Montana. Many froze to

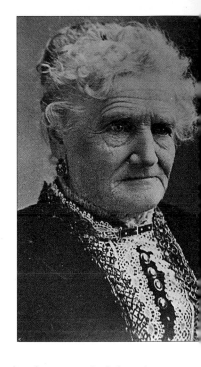

Esther Morris (above) was the country's first woman judge.

The Black Hills area is heavily wooded, hilly land in northeastern Wyoming and western South Dakota.

death on the trail. By 1880, Wyoming had few Indians. Most of them lived on the Wind River Reservation.

THE FORTY-FOURTH STATE: PROBLEMS AND PROGRESS

In 1890, Wyoming had enough people (60,000) to become a state. On July 10, 1890, Wyoming entered the Union as the forty-fourth state.

Almost right away, the state had trouble. Big ranchers were angry at small ranchers. The small ranchers fenced in their land. This cut off the large ranchers' cattle from watering holes. Large ranchers also accused small ranchers of "rustling" (stealing cattle).

The trouble boiled over into the Johnson County Cattle War of 1892. The owners of large ranches made a "dead list." On it were suspected rustlers. In April 1892, two men from the list were killed. This happened in Johnson County. Many small ranchers joined together to fight the big ranchers. But United States troops arrived. The war came to an end.

In 1899, trouble started between cattle ranchers and sheep ranchers. Cattle ranchers felt that sheep

did not leave enough grass for cattle. Gangs of masked cattle ranchers went on the attack. They killed thousands of sheep and about twenty sheep raisers. Three sheep ranchers were murdered near Ten Sleep in 1909. Five of their killers were jailed. The cattlemen then stopped their attacks. Wyoming's "Wild West" days ended.

As the cattle wars ended, more tourists came to Wyoming. Shoshone National Forest had been founded in 1902. Devils Tower National Monument had been created in 1906. These were the country's first national forest and national monument.

An early Wyoming sheepherder with his traveling house

Today, the United States has about 150 national forests and about 80 national monuments.

In 1912, oil become important to Wyoming. Oil gushed from the Salt Creek Field that year. Nearby Casper became an oil-refining center.

Many dams were built on Wyoming rivers in the 1900s. Buffalo Bill Dam was completed in 1910. Alcova and Seminoe dams were finished in the 1930s. Water stored behind the dams is sent to dry land. The dams opened more of Wyoming to farming.

In 1917, the United States entered World War I (1914-1918). More than 12,000 Wyomingites served. About 500 of them died winning the war. Their names are on a tablet at the capitol in Cheyenne.

The Great Depression (1929-1939) caused hard times in the United States. About 130 Wyoming banks failed. Many Wyomingites lost their ranches

Oil wells like this one became important to Wyoming in the early 1900s.

and farms. Many people found work building dams on Wyoming's rivers.

World War II (1939-1945) helped end the Great Depression. The United States entered the war in 1941. About 33,000 Wyoming men and women served in the war. The state's cattle supplied beef for the people in uniform. Oil, coal, and iron from Wyoming also helped win the war.

These residents of Kemmerer were collecting scrap for the war effort during World War II.

WYOMING AFTER WORLD WAR II

Two more treasures came from Wyoming's land after World War II. In 1947, mining of trona began around Green River. The country's largest trona deposit is there. Trona goes into making glass, paper, soaps, and baking soda. Green River became known as the "Trona Capital of the World." Uranium was found in the Powder River area in 1951. This metal is used in atomic bombs and nuclear reactors.

In the 1950s, Wyoming enjoyed a tourist boom. Vacationers flocked to Yellowstone and Grand Teton national parks. Many stayed at dude ranches. These are places where guests can ride horses and enjoy the Western life. By 1970, tourism was a giant business in Wyoming.

Grand Teton National Park was founded in 1929.

The 1970s and 1980s were like a roller-coaster ride for Wyoming. The 1970s were the "up" period. Oil prices rose. Workers in oil-related businesses moved to the state. In ten years, Wyoming's population climbed from 332,416 to 469,557. New homes and schools were built. In 1975, Wyoming's lawmakers created a special fund. It set aside billions of dollars in oil and mineral taxes. Those funds were to be used in tough times.

Those tough times arrived in the 1980s. During this "down" period, oil prices dropped by half. Uranium mines began to close. As jobs disappeared, thousands of people moved away. Wyoming's population dropped by more than 13,000.

Twenty-seven United States cities have more people than the whole state of Wyoming.

In 1988, disaster hit Yellowstone National Park. Fires raged through the park. Elk and buffalo were killed. Old buildings burned. About one-third of the park was damaged.

In 1989, Indians on the Wind River Reservation won a victory. The United States Supreme Court ruled that the Indians have water rights to the Wind River. The Shoshone and Arapaho are stocking the river with fish. They hope to attract people who enjoy fishing. Such tourists would bring much-needed business to the reservation.

28

The Equality State celebrated its 100th birthday in 1990. Since then, Wyomingites have had other reasons to celebrate. Wyoming's coal and natural gas production is on the rise. Taxes from natural gas pipelines help fund Wyoming's schools. As of 1993, Wyoming had one of the country's lowest jobless rates. One reason is because so many people had left the state. Since the 1988 fire, wildlife and flowers have returned to Yellowstone Park. The outlook for Wyoming's second 100 years is indeed bright.

In 1990, Cheyenne's annual Frontier Days celebration marked the state's 100th birthday.

Overleaf: A camper in the Teton Wilderness shows off her white trail cake.

WYOMINGITES AND THEIR WORK

Wyoming has the fewest people of the fifty states. The 1990 Census counted 453,588 Wyomingites. About 95 of every 100 Wyomingites are white. Hispanics are the largest minority. About 26,000 Wyomingites have Spanish-speaking backgrounds. Many of their families came from Mexico. Nearly 10,000 American Indians live in Wyoming. About half of them live on the Wind River Reservation. About 4,000 Wyomingites are black. Another 3,000 have Asian backgrounds.

Wyoming's largest cities have fewer people than some states' small towns. Wyomingites aren't crowded together. Perhaps that is why Wyoming's crime rate is low. The small population has another pleasant outcome. Wyomingites take pride in treating each person courteously.

THEIR WORK

About half of all Wyomingites have jobs. Government work is the state's leading type of job. National forests and parklands employ many of

These Southern Plains Indian dancers were about to entertain during Cheyenne's Frontier Days.

The United States government owns about half the land in Wyoming.

31

Wyoming's 55,000 government workers. Others work at Warren Air Force Base, outside Cheyenne.

Selling goods is the second-leading kind of work. About 45,000 Wyomingites do this. They sell such things as food, clothing, and cars. About 40,000 Wyomingites provide services. They include doctors, nurses, and lawyers. Employees of ski resorts and hotels are also service workers.

About 18,000 Wyomingites work in mining. Wyoming has the highest percentage of mine workers of any state. Wyoming is the number-one state for mining coal. About 400 billion pounds of coal are mined there each year. Only nine countries mine more coal than Wyoming. Wyoming also leads the country at mining trona and bentonite. Wyoming

The mining of coal is important in Wyoming. This open-pit coal mine is in Gillette.

ranks fourth in the country at producing oil. Wyoming is sixth at producing natural gas.

Wyoming has about 9,000 farms and ranches. They average 6 square miles in size. Only in Arizona are farms bigger. Beef cattle are Wyoming's top farm product. Sheep are important, too. They provide wool and meat. Wyoming ranks sixth in the United States at growing sugar beets. They are used to make sugar. Wyoming ranks ninth at harvesting dry beans. Wheat, corn, and hay are other Wyoming crops.

Wyoming ranks last in the United States at manufacturing. About 9,000 Wyomingites make goods. Soda ash, refined oil, and other chemicals are Wyoming's top products. Machinery, wood products, and printed material are also important.

These cattle are being rounded up for branding.

Wyoming ranks seventeenth in the United States at raising beef cattle. It is third behind only Texas and California at raising sheep.

Overleaf: Terraces at Mammoth Hot Springs in Yellowstone National Park

A Trip Through
the Equality State

A Trip Through the Equality State

About 7 million people visit Wyoming each year. This is over fifteen times the state's population. Visitors come to see Wyoming's geysers and waterfalls. They climb its mountains and raft down its rivers. The state's rodeos and historic sites also attract many people.

Cheyenne

Cheyenne is a good place to start a Wyoming tour. This city is near Wyoming's southeast corner. Cheyenne is the state capital. With 50,000 people, Cheyenne is also Wyoming's largest city.

A 146-foot-tall golden dome rises above Cheyenne. The dome tops the state capitol. Wyoming lawmakers meet in this building. Outside, two statues greet visitors. One is a statue of Esther Morris. The other statue is *The Spirit of Wyoming*. It shows a cowboy riding a bucking horse.

The Historic Governors' Mansion is another Cheyenne landmark. Wyoming's governors lived there from 1905 to 1976. A new governor's home

This statue of a cowboy on a bucking bronco stands outside the capitol, in Cheyenne.

was completed in 1976. The Wyoming State Museum has exhibits about Wyoming's early days.

Each July since 1897, Cheyenne has celebrated Frontier Days. There are parades with horse-drawn carriages. Country-and-western singers perform. A chuck-wagon breakfast is held. The world's biggest outdoor rodeo is the main event. The Cheyenne Frontier Days Old West Museum is on the rodeo grounds. Visitors can view displays on rodeo champions and rodeo clowns.

The old grandstand is crowded during Cheyenne's annual Frontier Days celebration.

OTHER SOUTHERN WYOMING HIGHLIGHTS

Northwest of Cheyenne is Laramie. This is Wyoming's third-biggest city. Almost 27,000 people live there. Laramie was once called "Hell-on-Wheels." Tough railroad crews gathered there. Today, Laramie is home to the University of Wyoming. It is the state's only four-year college. The school's teams are called the Cowboys and Cowgirls. The Laramie Plains Museum is in an old mansion. Its displays include toys, china, and lovely furniture. They are from the town's early years.

Flaming Gorge National Recreation Area is in southwest Wyoming. It also spills into Utah.

Left: The Laramie Plains Museum Right: The Union building, at the University of Wyoming campus, in Laramie

Flaming Gorge is a brilliant red canyon along the Green River. Water and wind carved the colorful rock formations. Visitors enjoy camping, hiking, and fishing in the area.

Rock Springs is north of Flaming Gorge. It has over 19,000 people. That makes Rock Springs Wyoming's fourth-biggest city. Each May the town hosts the Rocky Mountain All-Girl Rodeo. West of Rock Springs is the Granger Stage Station. It was a Pony Express stop. In 1860-61, the Pony Express delivered mail out West. Relays of riders on horseback carried the mail.

Farther west is Fossil Butte National Monument. It is near Kemmerer in southwest

Colorful Flaming Gorge and the Green River

Wyoming. About 50 million years ago, this butte was covered by water. Today, fish fossils are found in this tall rock.

ACROSS WYOMING'S MIDDLE THIRD

The Wind River Reservation covers 3,500 square miles. That is more land than the state of Delaware.

St. Stephens Mission, near Riverton

The Wind River Indian Reservation is in west central Wyoming. Many Shoshone and Arapaho make their homes there. They hold several yearly pow-wows. Indians from around the country attend these gatherings. They renew old friendships and customs. There are Indian dances, foods, and stories. Old games are played. The Shoshone enjoy the "hand game." A small object is passed around. The "guesser" has to figure out who has the object.

Riverton is in the reservation's southeast corner. But it is not part of the reservation. Riverton hosts the Cowboy Music and Poetry Festival each October. Long ago, cowboys sang to their cattle to calm them. Today's cowboys and cowgirls still write songs and poems. They are performed at the festival.

Thermopolis is near the reservation's northeast corner. Rocks within the earth heat underground water at Thermopolis. The water bubbles up as hot springs. People come to bathe in Thermopolis's

spring waters. The Hot Springs County Historical Museum has the bar from Thermopolis's Hole-in-the-Wall Saloon. Hole-in-the-Wall was an area south of Buffalo, Wyoming. Long ago, outlaws Butch Cassidy and the Sundance Kid hid out there. Cassidy is said to have hidden $70,000 in the Wind River Mountains. The money was never found.

East of Thermopolis is the 2,000-foot-deep Wind River Canyon. The Wind River carved this canyon. Hell's Half Acre is another canyon in central Wyoming. One part of it is called Devil's

Left: Hell's Half Acre
Right: Wind River Canyon

41

Kitchen. During the early 1800s, coal deposits there caught fire. They burned for many years.

Independence Rock is south of Hell's Half Acre. This 193-foot-tall rock was a rest stop on the Oregon Trail. Pioneers tried to reach it by July 4. If they did, their trip was on schedule. About 50,000 pioneers carved their names on the rock. Many of the names can still be seen.

Casper is east of Independence Rock. Begun in 1887, Casper today has about 47,000 people. It is Wyoming's second-largest city. Casper is called the "Oil Capital of the Rockies." Companies that mine

The city of Casper, with the North Platte River in the foreground and the Casper Mountains in the background

oil, natural gas, and coal are based there. Old Fort Caspar has been restored. Today, visitors can view exhibits about the Oregon Trail and the Pony Express.

Douglas is east of Casper. It hosts the Wyoming State Fair each summer. The Wyoming Pioneer Museum is also in Douglas. Displays range from rustlers' branding irons to ladies' fans. Visitors can also see an 1886 one-room school. Several dude ranches are located around Douglas.

Lusk is in far eastern Wyoming. It is near the Nebraska border. The Stagecoach Museum is at Lusk. A stagecoach that ran between Cheyenne and Deadwood, South Dakota, is there. Also of interest is a thirty-one star United States' flag from 1876.

NORTHERN WYOMING

Devils Tower is a natural wonder of northeast Wyoming. It is the country's oldest national monument. Millions of years ago, hot rock poured from the earth. It hardened into a 1,280-foot-tall tower.

Southeast of Devils Tower is Gillette. Many coal mines are located near Gillette. One is Thunder Basin Mine. It is the country's largest coal mine. The country's largest pronghorn antelope herd is

Devils Tower (above) is nearly the height of the world's tallest building. The Sears Tower in Chicago is 1,454 feet tall.

The Buffalo Bill Historical Center

A rainbow forms at the Lower Falls of the Grand Canyon of the Yellowstone River.

near Gillette. About 50,000 pronghorns are in the herd.

Buffalo is west of Gillette. It is the seat of Johnson County. Buffalo's Jim Gatchell Museum has displays on the Johnson County Cattle War. Sheridan is a short drive north of Buffalo. The Bradford Brinton Memorial Ranch is near Sheridan. The twenty-room ranch house is a museum of Western art and history.

West of Buffalo is Cody. William Cody founded the town in 1895. He was called Buffalo Bill. As a young man, Cody hunted buffalo to feed the railroad crews. Cody has four great Western museums. The Buffalo Bill Museum displays guns and saddles that belonged to Cody. The Whitney Gallery of Western Art has paintings and sculptures of the Old West. The Plains Indian Museum exhibits Native American tools and clothing. The Cody Firearms Museum traces the history of guns. The four museums make up the Buffalo Bill Historical Center.

Yellowstone National Park is in Wyoming's northwest corner. About 3 million people visit the country's oldest national park each year. The Yellowstone River runs through the park. Two big waterfalls are formed as the river drops into a canyon. The Lower Falls has a 308-foot drop. The

Upper Falls tumbles 109 feet. Yellowstone Lake is also in the park. It is the United States' highest natural freshwater lake.

Hot underground rocks create unusual sights at Yellowstone. Some cause pools of colorful mud to bubble like witches' brews. These are called paint pots. The park also has many hot springs. Mammoth Hot Springs is the best-known one. Its many levels of springs spill down over one another.

The park also has many geysers. From them, water explodes out of the ground. Yellowstone's "Old Faithful" is a world-famous geyser. Almost every 74 minutes, it shoots water about 130 feet

Old Faithful

Mineral deposits have formed terraces at Mammoth Hot Springs, in Yellowstone National Park.

An aspen grove in Grand Teton National Park

high. Yellowstone's Steamboat Geyser is the world's tallest geyser. It shoots water 400 feet.

Yellowstone's wildlife is another attraction. Grizzly bears, black bears, buffalo, and elk roam about. Bald eagles and swans nest near the park's lakes.

Grand Teton National Park is just south of Yellowstone. The park's Teton Mountains are among the country's youngest peaks. They are only 9 million years old. Grand Teton is the range's highest peak. It is also Wyoming's second-highest mountain. Grand Teton stands 13,770 feet high.

Jackson Hole is in Grand Teton National Park. "Hole" is an old mountain-man word. It means a

valley surrounded by mountains. Jackson Hole is huge. It is 50 miles long and 7 miles wide. The Teton Mountains rise above Jackson Hole.

Jackson is just outside Grand Teton National Park. It is a good place to end a tour of Wyoming. About 10,000 elk winter at the National Elk Refuge there. An arch of elk antlers marks the entrance to Jackson's town square. Jackson's sidewalks are wooden boardwalks. Handrails keep walkers from falling into the street. Wildlife of the American West is an art museum. Hundreds of paintings and sculptures of Western animals can be seen there. Jackson also has many art galleries. The scenery brings many artists to this part of Wyoming.

A view of the town of Jackson

An arch made of elk antlers, in Jackson

A Gallery of Famous Wyomingites

A Gallery of Famous Wyomingites

Many well-known Americans have lived in Wyoming. They include Indian chiefs, lawmakers, authors, and artists. **Washakie** (1804?-1900) was born in Montana. This Shoshone chief lived much of his life in Wyoming. Washakie was a mighty warrior. But he befriended the white people. He wanted to bring peace to his own people. In 1868, Washakie signed the Fort Bridger Treaty. It granted the Wind River Reservation to the Shoshone. Washakie is buried on the reservation.

Spotted Tail (1823?-1881) was born near Fort Laramie. He was a Sioux chief. Spotted Tail was also a great warrior. He, too, felt that his people should make peace with the whites. Other Sioux did not agree with him. Spotted Tail was killed by a Sioux warrior.

Jim Bridger (1804-1881) was born in Virginia. He was a trapper and explorer in the Rockies. He built Wyoming's Fort Bridger. He blazed many trails. Bridger helped people get through the mountains. Bridger Peak, Bridger Mountains, and Bridger National Forest were named for him.

Shoshone Chief Washakie

Opposite: Nellie Tayloe Ross

Robert D. Carey

Milward Simpson

Esther Morris (1814-1902) was born in New York. She moved to South Pass City about 1869. She soon became the country's first woman judge (1870). Statues of famous people from each state stand in the Capitol in Washington, D.C. Wyoming's statue is of Esther Morris.

Nellie Tayloe Ross (1876-1977) was born in Missouri. Later, she moved to Cheyenne. Her husband was Wyoming's governor William B. Ross. They had three sons. William died in office in 1924. Nellie was elected to finish his term (1925-1927). She became the country's first woman governor. Later, Ross became the first women director of the U.S. Mint (1933-1953). In that post, she oversaw the building of Fort Knox in Kentucky. That is where the government's gold is stored.

Two famous pairs of father-son lawmakers were Wyomingites. **Joseph Carey** (1845-1924) was the Wyoming Territory's representative to Congress. He wrote the bill that admitted Wyoming as a state. Later, he governed the state (1911-1915). His son was **Robert Carey** (1878-1937). He also served as Wyoming's governor (1919-1923). Later, he became a U.S. senator (1931-1936).

Milward Simpson (1897-1993) was born in Jackson. As governor (1955-1959), he helped expand the University of Wyoming. Later, he served in the U.S. Senate (1963-1969). **Alan Simpson**, his son, was born in Cody in 1931. Alan Simpson has served Wyoming in the U.S. Senate since 1978.

Harriett Elizabeth "Liz" Byrd was born in Cheyenne in 1926. She became Wyoming's first full-time black teacher. For twenty-seven years, she taught second grade in Cheyenne. Besides teaching, she served in the Wyoming legislature for twelve years. In 1985, Byrd's students at Deming School created a bill. It named the buffalo as the state mammal. Byrd sponsored another important bill. It requires Wyoming parents to place their babies in car safety seats.

John Clymer (1907-1987) was born in Washington. Later, he lived in Teton Village. He painted historical Western scenes. Three huge Clymer paintings hang in Cody's Whitney Gallery of Art. They are *The Cattle Drive*, *The Gold Train*, and *The Homesteaders*.

Jackson Pollock (1912-1956) was born in Cody. He had a different way of painting. Pollack called it action painting. He placed big canvases on the floor. Then, he splashed or dribbled paint on them. He even used a squirt gun. His paintings include *White Light* and *Easter* and the *Totem*.

Liz Byrd

John Clymer

Owen Wister

Grace Raymond Hebard

Wyoming has also produced some baseball stars. **Dick Ellsworth** was born in Lusk in 1940. He was a left-handed pitcher. In 1963, he won twenty-two games for the Chicago Cubs. **Tom Browning** is another left-handed pitcher. He was born in Casper in 1960. In 1988, Browning won eighteen games. He pitched the Cincinnati Reds' first perfect game.

Several fine authors have lived in Wyoming. **Owen Wister** (1860-1938) was born in Pennsylvania. He later moved to Wyoming. Wister wrote *The Virginian*. It is a cowboy novel set in Wyoming's Medicine Bow area. The book was made into four popular movies. "I have never enjoyed anything more than my days in Wyoming," Wister once said.

Grace Raymond Hebard (1861-1936) moved from Iowa to Wyoming. In 1914, she became the state's first woman lawyer. She also taught for many years at the University of Wyoming. Hebard is best-known for her books on Western history. One of them was a biography of Chief Washakie.

Patricia MacLachlan was born in Cheyenne in 1938. Later, she became a children's author. MacLachlan says that she talks to her characters as she writes. In that way, she breathes life into them. MacLachlan won the 1986 Newbery Medal for

Sarah, Plain and Tall. It is about a young woman who moves to the West to get married.

Tom Browning (above) pitched a perfect game for the Cincinnati Reds. In a perfect game, a pitcher allows no one to reach base.

The birthplace of Spotted Tail, Liz Byrd, Patricia MacLachlan, and Jackson Pollock . . .

Home also to Washakie, Jim Bridger, Esther Morris, and Nellie Tayloe Ross . . .

The first state to grant women full voting rights and the first to have a national park, national forest, and national monument . . .

Today, the top state at mining coal and trona. . .

This is Wyoming—the Equality State.

Did You Know?

In 1920-21, Jackson was the first United States town governed completely by women. Grace Miller was mayor. The town marshal and all four council members were also women. Rose Crabtree defeated her own husband for her council position.

Wyomingites often lean over to walk in the wind. They say that whenever the wind stops, a few of the leaning people fall to the ground.

Mr. T was called the greatest bucking rodeo bull in history. He threw 188 cowboys over five years. In 1989, at Cheyenne Frontier Days, Marty Staneart became the first person to ride Mr. T successfully.

Martha "Calamity Jane" Canary worked as a frontier scout in Wyoming. She once explained how she was nicknamed "Calamity," which means "trouble." A soldier was shot by Indians. Canary placed him on her horse and took him to an army post at present-day Sheridan. After recovering, the soldier told her: "I name you Calamity Jane, heroine of the plains."

Calamity Jane was credited with an old Wyoming recipe for "twenty-year cake." People said it could sit for twenty years and still be eaten!

Max Meyer ran a Cheyenne clothing store for sixty-one years, starting in the 1880s. He invented the "ten-gallon" cowboy hat. The hat was named for its great size.

Nellie Tayloe Ross's birthday, November 29, is a holiday in Wyoming.

Ralph Herrick of Douglas made up stories about the jackalope, a mythical Wyoming animal. The jackalope is supposed to have a rabbit's body and an antelope's antlers. There is a large sculpture of a jackalope in Douglas.

Gerald Ford, the thirty-eighth president of the United States, was a Yellowstone Park ranger as a young man.

In a famous 1941 stunt, George Hopkins parachuted onto Devils Tower. He was stranded there for six days before being rescued.

The fossil cabin is at southeast Wyoming's Como Bluff. It is made with dinosaur bones found at the bluff.

The Indians figured distances in "sleeps." This meant a day of travel and a night of sleep. The town of Ten Sleep was named because the Indians considered the site ten sleeps from Fort Laramie. Other unusual Wyoming town names include Chugwater, Sundance, West Thumb, and Bill.

Yellowstone Park's last wolf was killed in 1923. Recently, several wolves that may have come from Montana have been seen in the park. Some wildlife groups want to bring wolves back to Yellowstone.

WYOMING INFORMATION

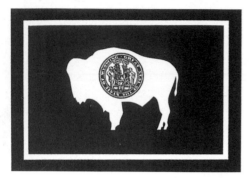

State flag

Meadowlark

Area: 97,809 square miles (the ninth-largest state)

Greatest Distance North to South: 275 miles

Greatest Distance East to West: 362 miles

Borders: Montana to the north; South Dakota and Nebraska to the east; Colorado and Utah to the south; Utah, Idaho, and Montana to the west

Highest Point: Gannett Peak in the Rocky Mountains, 13,804 feet above sea level

Lowest Point: 3,100 feet above sea level, along the Belle Fourche River in the state's northeast corner

Hottest Recorded Temperature: 115° F. (at Basin in northern Wyoming, on August 8, 1983, and at Diversion Dam on July 15, 1988)

Coldest Recorded Temperature: -63° F. (at Moran Junction in Grand Teton National Park, on February 9, 1933)

Statehood: The forty-fourth state, on July 10, 1890

Origin of Name: *Wyoming* is from Indian words meaning "large plains"; it was named after Pennsylvania's Wyoming Valley

Capital: Cheyenne

Counties: 23

United States Representatives: 1

State Senators: 30

State Representatives: 60

State Song: "Wyoming," by Charles E. Winter (words) and George E. Knapp (music)

State Motto: "Equal Rights"

Nicknames: "Equality State," "Cowboy State "

State Seal: Adopted in 1893

State Flag: Adopted in 1917

State Flower: Indian paintbrush

State Bird: Meadowlark

State Tree: Cottonwood

State Mammal: Buffalo (American bison)

State Fish: Cutthroat trout

State Insignia: Bucking horse

State Gemstone: Jade

State Fossil: Knightia (a fish)

Mountains: Rocky Mountains

Some Rivers: North Platte, Clarks Fork, Green, Sweetwater, Shoshone, Wind, Bighorn, Snake, Powder

Some Lakes: Yellowstone, Jackson, Shoshone, Flaming Gorge, Buffalo Bill

Wildlife: Buffalo, pronghorn antelopes, elk, moose, mule deer, white-tailed deer, bighorn sheep, mountain lions, black bears, grizzly bears, beavers, rabbits, prairie dogs, coyotes, bobcats, meadowlarks, grouse, bald eagles, swans, wild turkeys, many other kinds of birds, trout, bass, walleye, perch, many other kinds of fish, rattlesnakes, garter snakes, toads, frogs

Farm Products: Beef cattle, sheep, sugar beets, dry beans, wheat, corn, hay, barley

Mining Products: Coal, oil, natural gas, trona, bentonite and other clays, uranium, crushed stones, gypsum, sand and gravel

Manufactured Products: Chemicals, refined oil, sugar, meat, flour, wood products, printed material, glass goods, farm machinery, clothing

Population: 453,588, fiftieth among the states
(1990 U.S. Census Bureau figures)

Major Cities (1990 Census):

Cheyenne	50,008	Sheridan	13,900
Casper	46,742	Green River	12,711
Laramie	26,687	Evanston	10,903
Rock Springs	19,050	Rawlins	9,380
Gillette	17,635	Riverton	9,202

Indian paintbrush

Bison

Cottonwood

WYOMING HISTORY

10,000 B.C.—Prehistoric Indians arrive in Wyoming

1743—French-Canadian brothers François and Louis Joseph Vérendrye are thought to be the first non-Indians to reach Wyoming

1803—Wyoming becomes part of the United States through the Louisiana Purchase

1807—John Colter explores what is now Yellowstone National Park

1812—Robert Stuart discovers South Pass

1825—William Ashley holds the first rendezvous for fur trappers

1834—William Sublette and Robert Campbell build Fort William (later named Fort Laramie), Wyoming's first permanent non-Indian settlement

1842—Jim Bridger begins building Fort Bridger

1854—Thirty U.S. soldiers are killed by Indians in the Grattan Massacre east of Fort Laramie

1865—Caspar Collins is killed at the Battle of Platte Bridge, near present-day Casper

1866—Forts Phil Kearny and Reno are built; eighty-one men are killed in the Fetterman Fight

1867—In the Wagon Box Fight, soldiers and timber cutters fight off Sioux and Cheyenne warriors; gold is found at South Pass; Cheyenne is founded; the Union Pacific enters Wyoming

1868—The Fort Laramie Treaty is signed; Laramie is founded; the Wyoming Territory is created

1869—The Wyoming Territory's legislature passes the first law in the United States to grant women full voting rights

1872—Yellowstone becomes the first U.S. national park

1876—Major fighting in Wyoming between Indians and soldiers ends

The Carter Schoolhouse was Wyoming's first school. It stands at Fort Bridger State Historic Site.

1883—Wyoming's first oil well is drilled

1887—The University of Wyoming opens in Laramie

1890—On July 10, Wyoming becomes the forty-fourth state

1892—The Johnson County Cattle War breaks out

1899-1909—Cattle ranchers and sheep ranchers fight to control grazing lands

1902—Shoshone, the first U.S. national forest, is founded in Wyoming

1903—An explosion at Hanna kills 169 miners in Wyoming's deadliest coal-mine disaster

1906—Devils Tower becomes the first U.S. national monument

1912—The Salt Creek Field near Casper begins gushing oil

1917-18—About 12,000 Wyomingites help win World War I

1925—Nellie Tayloe Ross takes office as the country's first woman governor

1924-39—Wyoming ranchers suffer during a long depression

1941-45—After the United States enters World War II, about 33,000 Wyoming men and women serve their country

1947—Trona mining begins around Green River, which becomes the "Trona Capital of the World"

1951—Uranium is discovered in Wyoming

1959—An earthquake strikes Yellowstone National Park

1960—Warren Air Force Base outside Cheyenne becomes a launch center for the U.S. guided missile system

1975—Wyoming lawmakers create a fuel tax reserve

1988—Forest fires burn about one-third of Yellowstone National Park; Wyoming becomes the country's top coal producer

1990—Wyoming's population is 453,588; on July 10, Wyoming celebrates its 100th birthday as a state

1992—A natural gas pipeline linking Wyoming and California opens

The Union Pacific railyards at Green River, the Trona Capital of the World

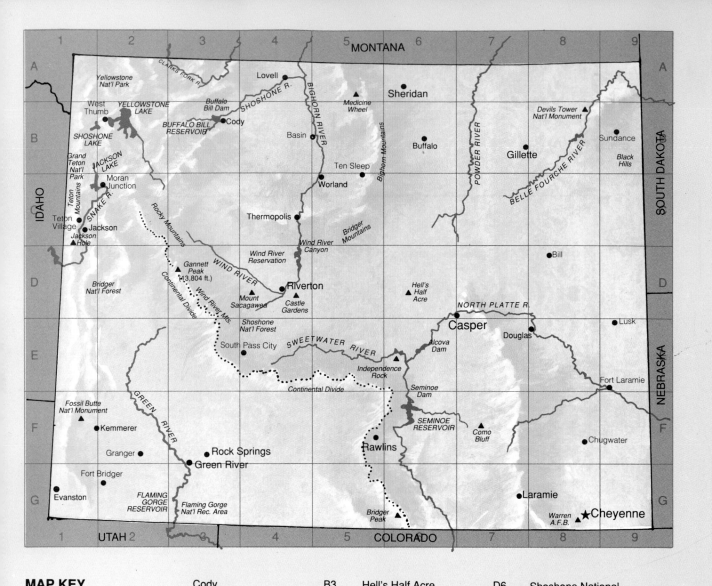

MAP KEY

GLOSSARY

ancestor: A person from whom other persons are descended, such as a great-grandparent

ancient: Relating to a time early in history

billion: A thousand million (1,000,000,000)

blizzard: A snowstorm driven by very high winds

canyon: A deep, steep-sided valley

capital: The city that is the seat of government

capitol: The building in which a governing body meets

climate: The typical weather of a region

colony: A settlement that is outside a parent country and that is ruled by the parent country

dinosaur: Generally, a huge animal that died out millions of years ago

dude ranch: A Western resort that offers activities such as horseback riding

explorer: A person who visits and studies unknown lands

fossil: The remains of an animal or a plant that lived long ago

geyser: Heated water that shoots up from the ground

hail: Balls of ice

mammoth: A prehistoric animal that looked much like today's elephants

mansion: A large, fancy house

manufacturing: The making of products

million: A thousand thousand (1,000,000)

pioneer: A person who is among the first to move into a region

population: The number of people in a place

powwow: A get-together of American Indians

rendezvous: A meeting place, or a gathering

reservation: Land in the United States that has been set aside for American Indians

reservoir: An artificially made lake where water is stored

rodeo: A contest in which cowboys and cowgirls ride horses and rope cattle

rustle: A term meaning to steal cattle

territory: Land owned by a country; with a capital "T" as in Wyoming Territory, it means a region with its own government that is owned by a country

PICTURE ACKNOWLEDGMENTS

Front cover, © **Tom Dietrich**; 1, © **Tom Dietrich**; 2, **Tom Dunnington**; 3, © Peter Cole/**N E Stock Photo**; 5, **Tom Dunnington**; 6-7, © M. Schneiders/**H. Armstrong Roberts**; 8, © **Tom Dietrich**; 9 (left), © **Bob & Suzanne Clemenz**; 9 (right), **Courtesy of Hammond, Incorporated, Maplewood, New Jersey**; 10, © Willard Clay/**Dembinsky Photo Assoc.**; 11, © **Tom Dietrich**; 12, © Biedel/**Photri, Inc.**; 13, © Mary A. Root/**Root Resources**; 14 (left), © P. Degginger/**H. Armstrong Roberts**; 14 (right), **Stock Montage, Inc.**; 16, **Denver Public Library, Western History Department**; 17, © **Cameramann International, Ltd.**; 18, **Denver Public Library, Western History Department**; 19, © W. J. Scott/**H. Armstrong Roberts**; 20, **Stock Montage, Inc.**; 21, **Wyoming State Museum**; 22, **Wyoming State Museum**; 23, **Stock Montage, Inc.**; 25, **North Wind Picture Archives**; 26, **Wyoming State Museum**; 27, **Wyoming State Museum**; 29, **Wyoming State Museum**; 30, © Bannock/**Photri, Inc.**; 31, © **Cameramann International, Ltd.**; 32, © **Cameramann International, Ltd.**; 33, © Sandra Nykerk/**Dembinsky Photo Assoc.**; 34-35, © Tom Dietrich/**H. Armstrong Roberts**; 36, © W.J. Scott/**H. Armstrong Roberts**; 37, © **Tom Dietrich**; 38 (left), © W.J. Scott/**H. Armstrong Roberts**; 38 (right), © **Tom Dietrich**; 39, © Ruth A. Smith/**Root Resources**; 40, © **Tom Dietrich**; 41 (both pictures), © **Tom Dietrich**; 42, © **Tom Dietrich**; 43, © **Tom Dietrich**; 44 (top), © **Photri, Inc.**; 44 (bottom), © Richard T. Nowitz/**Photri, Inc.**; 45 (top), © **Tom Dietrich**; 45 (bottom), © **Tom Till**; 46, © Willard Clay/**Dembinsky Photo Assoc.**; 47 (top), © Roger Bickel/**N E Stock Photo**; 47 (bottom), © **Tom Dietrich**; 48, **AP/Wide World Photos**; 49, **Wyoming State Museum**; 50 (both pictures), **AP/Wide World Photos**; 51 (top), **Wyoming State Museum**; 51 (bottom), **UPI/Bettmann**; 52 (top), **AP/Wide World Photos**; 52 (bottom), **Wyoming State Museum**; 53, **AP/Wide World Photos**; 54, **Buffalo Bill Historical Center**; 55 (top), © **Dave Stoecklein Photography**; 55 (bottom), **Wyoming Division of Tourism**; 56 (top), **Courtesy Flag Research Center, Winchester, Massachusetts 01890**; 56 (bottom), © Rod Planck/**Dembinsky Photo Assoc.**; 57 (top), © Kitty Kohout/**Root Resources**; 57 (middle), © Stan Osolinski/**Dembinsky Photo Assoc.**; 57 (bottom), © **Jerry Hennen**; 58, © W.J. Scott/**H. Armstrong Roberts**; 59, © **Tom Dietrich**; 60, **Tom Dunnington**; back cover, © **Tom Dietrich**

INDEX

Page numbers in boldface type indicate illustrations.

ABOUT THE AUTHORS

Dennis and Judith Fradin have coauthored several books in the From Sea to Shining Sea series. The Fradins both graduated from Northwestern University in 1967. Dennis has been a professional writer for twenty years, and has published 150 books. His works for Childrens Press include the Young People's Stories of Our States series, the Disaster! series, and the Thirteen Colonies series. Judith earned her M.A. in literature from Northwestern University and taught high-school and college English for many years. The Fradins, who are the parents of Anthony, Diana, and Michael, live in Evanston, Illinois.